Website for Book

www.cambridgememorymanual.com

Clinical Website

www.londonmemoryclinic.com

Acknowledgements

I would like to thank colleagues past and present for their assistance in putting together this booklet. I would also like to thank the memory scientists and clinicians whose research has helped to generate some of the ideas outlined here, and the patients from whom I have learned so much.

About This Booklet

Memory lapses affect us all, young and old, able-bodied and disabled. This booklet is intended to offer advice on improving everyday memory skills, on helping to prevent memory lapses in the first place, and on trying to cope better with memory difficulties when they do occur. You may find that only some of the advice is suitable for your particular needs, or that you have to adapt any advice to your particular circumstances. It is important that you keep in mind that the advice in the booklet is meant to offer general guidelines, rather than a ready remedy for memory difficulties, and that the advice needs to be thought through before applying to your particular circumstances or to those of someone you know. This booklet is not meant to be a substitute for professional advice or treatment.

Contents

Play Shark Attack Memory Game

App Store QR code

Google Play QR code

1. What is Memory?

Memory is usually about retaining information and being able to bring it to mind. Having a good memory or a poor memory does not necessarily mean that other skills or abilities will also be affected. Remember the absent-minded professor who knows so much but who keeps forgetting where he has put things!

Different Types of Memory

There are different types of memory skills rather than a single memory ability. For example, remembering a name that you have just heard for the first time is different from remembering the name of your primary school.  Also, remembering how to drive a car is different from recalling an event from a recent holiday. Memory for skills such as driving a car may often be unaffected in people with everyday memory difficulties. Remembering things that happened many years ago is usually easier than remembering something that happened yesterday, partly because older memories may be especially meaningful and tend to be rehearsed over and over again.

Trying to find the right word while having a conversation, such as remembering what something is called, is also a form of memory difficulty, but one which cannot be easily improved and is not covered in detail in this manual. If you are in such a situation, try to stay calm and – if it is possible - wait for a while, since the word may come back to you. Going through letters of the alphabet or thinking of other associations may also help to bring the word to mind.

Different Stages of Remembering

When we remember something for the first time, there are usually three stages involved. The *learning* stage - what happens when we concentrate on something for the first time, regularly rehearse it afterwards, etc. The *storage* stage - when things we've learned are stored in the brain. The *recall* stage - when we try to bring to mind what we've learned. If any of these stages is affected, then a memory lapse may occur. While there is usually little we can do directly to greatly improve the *storage* stage of memory, we can usually do something about the *learning* and *recall* stages. Much of this manual is about offering advice and suggestions as to how you may try to improve your learning and recall skills.

Things to Bear in Mind

No one's memory is perfect! We all tend to forget things from time to time. Having a memory problem does not mean that you are 'stupid' or 'going crazy'. You may find it useful to keep a diary for a few days of your memory lapses - this will help you see that in fact your memory may not be all that bad. It may also help pinpoint those areas of your memory that you need to work on, and whether your memory lapses are due to factors such as tiredness, stress or doing too many things at once. What stays in our memory will often depend on a number of factors –

- **How much time was spent during the experience** – the longer the time, the more likely that the memory will stick

- **How distinct the event or experience was** – the more distinct and unique that it was, the more likely that it will be retained

- **How novel and unexpected it was** – the more novel and the more of a surprise, the more likely that it will be remembered

- **How personally relevant it was** – the more that the event or items were personally meaningful, and the more that they can be linked to related knowledge and experiences, the more likely that they will be retained in memory

- **How emotionally charged was the event** – the more emotional the event, either positive or negative, the more likely that it will be remembered

- **How often it was repeated** – if the event or item was repeated on several instances, or regularly brought to mind on a number of occasions, then it is more likely that it will have a stronger impression on one's memory

- **How visual the memory was** – generally, pictures and colourful images are more likely to have an impact on memory than spoken or written words

You may well find you are now more aware of memory lapses, compared to a few years ago, but it is important to realise that your memory was never perfect. You shouldn't say things to yourself such as *"My memory is hopeless"* or *"I'm stupid, I'm always forgetting things"* because this may make you feel that your memory is worse than it actually is. If you really are forgetful lots of times, try to keep a sense of humour about it. Coping with memory lapses, by staying calm and patient, and by being open about any memory difficulties, is as important a skill to develop as improving memory in the first place.

Try to be well organized in your everyday routine. This may mean only doing certain things at certain times of the day or on certain days of the week, putting things away or filing things carefully in their own place, not allowing the place where you work or live to get cluttered, labelling cupboards, drawers, files, etc.

A poor memory is sometimes the result of poor concentration or trying to do too many things at once. This may result in 'absent-minded' memory lapses such as forgetting what you went into a room for, forgetting where you put things, and forgetting to turn items on or off. When you are doing one thing, try to concentrate on it and don't let your mind wander on to other things. You will learn best in a place that is mostly free of distractions. When you find such a place, get into the habit of using it regularly. If you are motivated to remember or learn something, it will help your concentration enormously, so try to think of ways to improve your motivation if something initially appears to be rather boring.

 Life style and your physical and mental well-being can affect concentration which in turn can affect your memory. Your memory will play up if you are under stress or anxiety, if you suffer from poor sleep or fatigue, if you are in pain, if you drink alcohol to excess or take recreational drugs, or if you are taking lots of medications, especially those which affect your brain. You may find that if you have a more healthy life-style with regular exercise and good weight control, and that if you are more relaxed about things and have a more easy-going routine, this itself may help to improve your memory.

It is important to remember that being more forgetful is a normal part of growing older. Even someone in their 30s will not have as good a memory as someone in their 20s.

Memory games, whether they be board games or computer-based 'brain training' exercises, can be fun to do and can sometimes be useful as a means for trying out various memory strategies. However, in themselves they are unlikely to make a major difference to everyday memory lapses of the type that are described in this manual. So, do not expect that memory exercises themselves will be a treatment for any memory difficulties that you may experience.

This booklet is intended to be a general guide to ways of improving memory, and not a "cure" for memory problems. At the moment, there are no drugs or treatments that will result in a big improvement in someone's memory. In each section of this manual, we'll be talking about three main ways in which you can help to improve your memory

- *Using Memory Aids*
- *Learning in Better Ways*
- *Recalling in Better Ways*

Using memory aids is one of the best ways to reduce the number of everyday memory lapses. Some people are worried that using such aids is a form of 'cheating' or that their brain will become 'lazy', or that others will look down on them, but this is far from the case. By contrast, using aids will mean that you are better organized, that you will be admired for this, and that using aids will often free up your mind to do other things more effectively.

2. Remembering To Do Something

Using Memory Aids

It is possible to think of three 'memory centres' that you will find useful for tasks such as remembering to do things – a 'home memory centre', a 'work memory centre', and a 'portable memory centre'. At home, try to set aside a particular place that you have as your 'home memory centre', where you keep your reminders – perhaps a dry whiteboard, calendar, diary, day-date clock, medication boxes, etc. A 'work memory centre' may be similar, but will have items that are key to remembering things in relation to your job; it will naturally be limited by the space you have in your workplace. A 'portable memory centre' will usually consist of a mobile phone, but for some people it may be a diary, a tablet/iPad or a laptop computer.

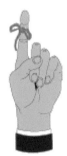

It is usually helpful to have 'prompts' which will help to remind you of things you have to do. For example, if you have to take something from home to get repaired, place it near the front door so that you can't help but see it when you leave the house. Or, if you always look in the hall mirror before you go out, stick a Post-it note on the mirror to remind you to take the thing with you.

Since regular Post-it notes may fall off after a while, it is useful to know that you can get ones that are 'super sticky' and will stick to a surface for longer. If you have to drop off something or someone when driving, keep a 'super sticky' Post-it notepad handy in the car, and put a note on the side window and/or dashboard to remind you to carry out that action. You can also buy mini pen-pads that can be attached inside a car, and can be used for quickly writing down a reminder.

Some people find that they may remember to do something later on if they have an unusual cue to remind them, such as a watch on the other hand, or small Post-it note stuck to the back of a hand. If you are at work, and need to remember to do something when you get home, write it down on a Post-it note, and attach it to something that you will definitely be looking at when you reach home.

If you keep forgetting to turn equipment off, have a sign on sticky tape next to the equipment to remind you to do this. If you leave taps running, have an overflow alarm device in place, or put a written reminder next to the tap, or just get into the habit of never leaving a room while the tap is running.

 Most mobile phones and similar devices will allow you to attach a message to a reminder alarm. It is now also possible to buy mobile phones and smartwatches into which you can enter things you have to do - when the alarm goes off, they will also show the message you entered. Some companies also offer a service whereby they will send a message to a mobile phone or computer on a set date or at regular times.

You can also buy pillboxes, with the days of the week and times of the day written on them, to help you remember to take tablets regularly.

Many people find it useful to have a dry whiteboard in a prominent place and to use it for writing down things that they have to do. The board could be divided into various sections - e.g. regular things to do, such as rubbish/garbage disposal, one-off events such as appointments, messages to/from someone, and important items of information such as key telephone numbers. You could write down messages in black, and circle in red those that are particularly important or urgent.

Keeping a diary, a wall-chart or wall-calendar is an obvious help in remembering to do something. If you keep a diary, check it regularly – say, before breakfast, just before lunch or last thing at night – both to write down the things that you have to do and to cross out the things that you have done. If you wish to check the diary more often, you could buy a watch with an hourly chime, and use the chime as a reminder to check your diary. If you keep a wall-calendar, hang it somewhere you look at most times of the day. If you have a diary keep this in a prominent place. If there is a list of birthdays or anniversaries you need to remember, it is a good idea to write all of these on a calendar at the beginning of the year.

Using Post-it notes, Post-it tape, or a little notebook for writing reminders is something that most people find useful. It is important when you think of something you have to do later on, that you write that thing down immediately in your diary or notebook rather than leaving it for another time. Keep a pencil and paper handy at your bedside in case, during the night, you suddenly think of something important that you have to do. In the morning, attend to this thing immediately after you get up, otherwise you may forget about it in the morning rush if you have to go to work.

If you are going on holiday somewhere, write down a list of things that you have to take. If you have a dry whiteboard, you could use this to write a list. Tick off the things as you pack them, and take a final look at the list when you are about to leave home. If you are often leaving things behind at home put a note permanently on the mirror or the front door to remind you to take everything with you. Whether you are leaving home to go on holiday, leaving a hotel room to return from holiday, or just leaving a bus or train, try to get into the habit to *'Look before you leave'* – have a quick look back and check that you have left nothing behind.

 Try carrying out a new, 'fragile' activity *before* a regular, 'fixed' habit – 'fragile before fixed'. Thus, if you need to take tablets, do it *before* something you regularly do – e.g. brushing your teeth in the morning, having a cup of tea in the morning, watching a TV programme in the evening, etc., or keep the tablets near your toothbrush, kettle or television to jog your memory. In general, try to get into a routine to do things at set times in the day - perhaps with one thing always following on from another. Also try to get into the habit of doing certain activities on set days of the week.

Learning in Better Ways

 Try to get into the habit of doing things *immediately* rather than after a while - if you leave things until later, you are more likely to forget to do them and they will be lost from your memory. Think of the motto – DO IT NOW. If you have to do several things at around the same time, count them up and remember the number of things to do if you count them off as you do them, you are less likely to leave one undone.

When you are thinking about something you have to do, try to get into the habit of saying it over to yourself several times. Space apart the times when you repeat the thing in question. If you have to do something on a later occasion, try to decide a particular time and particular place where you will carry out the action, rather than just any time in the future.

It may also be useful to make associations relating to the particular activity. For example, if you have to remember to go to the bakery after you go to the bank, you could make a picture in your mind of the bank clerk giving you a cake instead of money! If you have to remember to do something in a particular place, picture the place in your mind and imagine doing the thing in question. For example, if you have to remember to post a letter when you are near a shop, imagine the shop and picture yourself posting the letter when you are walking outside the shop. In general, it is easier to remember to do things if you make links between the things you have to do. If you have a number of things you have to say - as in a short speech you have to make - try to make some link between them.

If you have a long list of things to get, for example food to buy in a supermarket, and you don't have time to write things down on a piece of paper, try to group them together in some meaningful way. For example, vegetables could go together, cheese milk and butter could go together as they are all dairy products, and so on. Or you could think of the places in the supermarket where they are kept and try to link together those that are kept in the same area.

Sometimes it is easy to forget something after only a few seconds - for example, some toast you put back to reheat in the toaster. Try repeating a key word slowly to yourself ('*toast*'). By the time you have said it 10 times it should be time to check the toaster again.

If you lead a very busy life, try to get into the habit of regularly thinking about things that you have to do, or checking a list you have made. This way, you are more likely to keep them in your mind. If you regularly review your diary at set times, for example when you start work in the morning, after lunch, etc. this will help you to keep them in your mind so that they are less likely to be forgotten.

Recalling in Better Ways

Usually you will be unaware at the particular time that you have forgotten to do something. Occasionally, however, you may find that you realise that there is something that you have to do, but have forgotten exactly what it is. If you find yourself in this type of situation, stop and think for a moment about similar things you have to do - e.g. if you have forgotten what to buy while out shopping, think of other bits of shopping you were supposed to get. Try also to think back to the situation where you first thought about doing the item in question, or - if it is possible - go back to the place where you first decided to do the particular thing.

 People often forget whether or not they have already carried out a particular activity (e.g. shut a window, turned off an oven or a light). One way to help this type of memory is to make the memory more distinctive – add a sound to the memory by coughing or by saying aloud what you are doing. So, when you are turning the light off, you could then tap it once, and also say the words, *'That's the light off.'*

3. Remembering What People Tell You

Using Memory Aids

 Writing down what people tell you is an obvious memory aid. If it is a short message or shopping list, you could use a Post-it note. For keeping a daily record of events that have happened, such as meeting up with people, it may be useful to keep a diary that you check over on a regular basis. A diary could also be used for more immediate needs, such as remembering messages, especially if it is part of a Filofax system where there are separate pages for writing down messages. If you forget phone messages, have a message pad and pen next to the phone.

Having something like a dry-wipe whiteboard in a prominent place at home or at work provides a handy place for noting messages, such as things that you have been told. When you write things down, try to do this in an organized, meaningful way. Thus, you could split a long message under several main headings and number these. You could also make parts of the message stand out by simple techniques such as underlining, using capital letters or different coloured ink with a multi-coloured biro pen.

If you have a smartphone with a voice recorder, this may be handy for keeping a record of any messages. This may come in useful when someone is giving you directions or if you wish to record advice given by a doctor during a consultation. Some digital Dictaphones or voice recorder apps allow you to store messages in different files, so that one file can be used for home messages, another file for work messages, etc. Many mobile phones have voice recording features that can be used for storing messages or things to do.

Learning in Better Ways

When you are told something that you have to remember, try to think about what you were told – repeat it back in your own words, ask questions about what was said or think about whether you like/dislike what you heard. In general, the more you think about something when you first hear it or read it, the better it will stick in your memory.

When you have to remember numbers, try to join them into a group (e.g. remember 3-7-4 not as 'three-seven-four' but as 'three hundred and seventy four'). In the case of a long telephone number you may find it useful to make associations using the numbers. For example, you could try to remember a number such as 193852 as 19 x 2 = 38, followed by the number of weeks in the year (52). Similarly, 330 could be remembered as tea-time (3:30pm).

Grouping numbers together like this or finding meaning in them makes them less likely to be forgotten, especially if you re-organize the numbers in a way that is personally meaningful to you. This technique applies equally to other situations - e.g. remembering post-codes, zip numbers for addresses in USA, car registration numbers, etc.

In the case of a list of things, a useful technique is to form a word from the first letter of the items. For example, if you had to remember to buy Bread, Eggs, Dates and Soap you could remember that the letters B, D and E rhyme. Alternatively, you could form a link word out of the first letters of the items. In this example, the link word could be 'BEDS'. Then, by simply going through the letters of the 'link word' you could recall each of the shopping items.

It might also be useful to actually associate the 'link word' with the place you are going to, so that you don'  forget what you learned the key word for. Ir this example, you could make a picture ir your mind of some BEDS in front of the entrance to the supermarket you were goinç to. Another similar idea is to form links between the words in a list. So if you had tc remember to buy *brown bread, eggs, dates* and *soap,* you coulc imagine yourself making an *egg & date sandwich with browr bread,* and then washing your hands with *soap.*

An idea that you may find useful is to repeat a message severa times, at increasing intervals after you have initially heard it – e.g after 10 seconds, 30 seconds, 2 minutes and 5 minutes. This technique is sometimes known as 'expanding spaced rehearsal' Repeating it immediately afterwards will be useful, especially tc make sure you were listening carefully and you heard it properly but it is usually better if, on further occasions, you repeat the message after an interval during which you have been doing something else. Of course you may well find that if you try to repea it after too long an interval, you will actually have forgotten part o it. Therefore, it may be useful to arrange the intervals so that the only gradually increase in length.

Recalling in Better Ways

If you find that you have forgotten a particular message which has been given to you, stay calm. Try and think about othe things to do with the message – who gave it, where it wa given, what you were doing at the time and any simila messages you received at the time. You may find this help to bring the message back to mind. Try to bring to mind an associations you may have used to remember the items at the time.

4. Remembering People's Names

Using Memory Aids

There are no simple aids for dramatically improving your memory for people's names. If there are a number of people whose names you have to remember, you could try writing down their names in your diary or notebook, or in a particular part of your mobile phone. Putting down what each person does alongside the name may also help. Going over the names from time to time will be beneficial, especially if at the same time you try to picture the person's face. Most mobile phones allow you to store photographs of faces along with names, and such devices could be used to help you regularly rehearse people's names or regularly test yourself by trying to recall the name from the photo or from related information that you have stored.

Learning in Better Ways

When you meet someone for the first time, listen carefully to their name. If it's an unusual name ask them to spell it for you. If you are introduced to several people, try to make an excuse to repeat their names back to them (e.g. *"Let me be sure I've got your name right"*). Try to use the name as often as possible in your initial conversation (e.g. *"I'm glad to meet you, John. What work do you do, John?"*). It will probably help if you repeat the name again after a short interval, say after a few minutes, rather than immediately and gradually increase the interval before you repeat the name again. You may feel strange saying the person's name again and again in a conversation, but most people enjoy hearing their name being spoken!

If you can make some associations to the person's name or can get some other sort of meaning from the name, this will help you to remember it better. In the case of a foreign name, you may have to alter the way it sounds to make it more meaningful (e.g. *Mustafa* can become *Must Have A*). In some cases, the name may be easy to picture in your mind as something else (e.g. *Mr Butcher*), but in other cases you may have to twist the name slightly to make it sound more meaningful, e.g. *jam* for 'James' and *cone* for 'Cohen'.

If you are trying to remember both the first and second names, or the names of a couple of people, you may find it useful to form a word (one that you can easily picture) from the initial letters of the two names - e.g. for *Harry Thompson*, you could form the word HaT, and imagine the person wearing a hat, or for Mary and Peter you could make up the word MaP, and imagine them both reading a map.

One technique that may be a little difficult to learn and is therefore not suitable for everyone, is to make an unusual link between a mental image and the person's name. For example, if the person's name was *James Cohen*, you could imagine him eating from an ice-cream cone with jam on the top, and so when you meet the person next you would think of jam on an ice-cream cone and then think of the name *James* ('jam') *Cohen* ('cone')! Don't worry about making up an unusual picture - the more unusual it is, the more likely it is that the name will stick in your memory.

If the person has something unusual about his appearance you could associate this with his name - e.g. in the case of a *Mr. Cohen* if he has a beard you could imagine the beard being in the shape of a cone.

In general, concentrating on anything unusual about the person's face, or thinking how attractive the face is to you, should help to make it stick better in your memory, whether you want to learn their name or just that you've seen them before. Remember to concentrate on their face or physical appearance, rather than on things such as their dress or hairstyle, as these can change over time!

It may also be helpful to link the person with someone who has the same name and whom you know well - this could be one of your friends or a famous personality. Try to think of some similarities - e.g. in occupation or appearance - between the person who you are meeting for the first time and the other person you already know well. For example, if someone is called *Peter Shakespeare*, you could think of the name Shakespeare and try to think of some similarity between the person's appearance or occupation and that of the famous English playwright, William Shakespeare.

When you say good-bye to someone, try to make a habit of saying his or her name again (e.g. *"It was nice meeting you, John"*). Try to recall their face and name a short while later, and try to do this if possible every few hours and over the next few days. If you used any technique for learning to associate the face with the name, try to think of that technique when you are rehearsing the name.

If you have to remember a lot of names, for example work colleagues, members of a club, etc. it is worth trying to bring their faces and names to mind when you have a spare moment. It may also be worth keeping a note of their name in a diary, note-book or mobile phone, together with any other information about them.

Recalling in Better Ways

When you find you cannot remember a person's name, try not to panic! Try going through possible names beginning with each letter of the alphabet. Think of where you first learned the name and anything that you may have associated with the name. Don't give up immediately after trying to remember the name - if you try again later, it may come back to you.

If after trying a number of times you still can't recall the name, don't be afraid to ask the person his or her name - you could say something like - *'I remember you very well, but your name has slipped my mind for the moment.'* Or you could say your own name as you shake hands with the person. He or she may instinctively do the same when they shake hands with you. Finally, don't forget that you can often have a friendly chat with someone without actually saying their name!

5. Remembering Where You Put Something

Using Memory Aids

Electronic tagging devices are available that can be attached to an item that you may tend to lose, such as keys or a TV remote control. When you press a button on an electronic transmitter or a panel on a smartphone app, you will get a signal that helps you locate the missing item. Some electronic devices will also give out a signal when you are more than a certain distance away from an object, and this may help if you are often losing things by leaving them behind, such as a mobile phone.

If you are always losing something important, see if it can be attached to a cord 'necklace' or something that you always wear, such as a belt.

Try to be well organized about where you put things. Have set places in your home or office for specific things you use - e.g. everyday things (keys, purse, glasses, etc.), letters, etc. If you put items in a bowl, make sure it is a transparent, glass bowl and keep it in a prominent place. Try to get into the habit of putting things away carefully and returning them to their proper place after use. Spend some time (e.g. half an hour each Saturday morning) making things a little more organized and putting back things that may have been moved out of place.

It can be helpful to put labels onto cupboards or jars where you tend to keep particular things. For keeping some items, you might find it handy to have a plastic, see-through container with its own little drawers - such as you find in hardware or DIY stores.

It's a good idea to put small self-adhesive labels, with a name and telephone number, on certain things such as umbrellas or mobile phones that you tend to leave lying around. In fact, anything that can be lost or mislaid should have a label on i ('If you can lose it, label it'). For things such as coats, gloves, etc it is usually possible to buy pens or stamps that can write or prin a name and telephone number, or cloth labels that can be sewr into or ironed onto parts of a garment. If you are worried abou putting your home phone number, you could put your work numbe or that of a family member or friend who agrees to be contacted.

If you are out shopping, try to carry things together in a single bag

or briefcase. If you are carrying several bags see if you can put some inside each other - the fewer bags you have to carry, the less likely you are to leave one somewhere. Also, if you si down and put something like an umbrella or a bag near you, put it in front of you so that you can easily see it - you are then less likely to leave it behind. If you are putting items on the luggage rack of a train, it is a good idea to put them in front on the rack opposite to where you are sitting, so that they are within your view. If you are carrying several things around with you, keep in your mind the exact number of things you have, and then check from time to time that you still have the correct number of items.

If you tend to forget where you have parked your car, try to get into the habit of parking it in a regular place. If you park it in a car park try to park it near some part that sticks out, such as a sign or a pa kiosk. When you leave the car, note down the floor level and an other information that will help you find it again. When you are walking away from your car, glance back at it a few times and concentrate on where you left it. Some cars can be fitted with a remote control alarm system, so that when you press the remote control button from a distance the car horn will sound and the indicators will flash.

Learning in Better Ways

Be extra alert in situations where you are likely to leave things lying around – e.g. when travelling about, on buses or trains, in shops, etc. We often lose things or forget where we put things as a result of poor concentration or not being well organized. Stop and think each time you put something away. Concentrate for a few seconds and look at the particular place where you put the thing, and say out loud where you have put it. Also, try to give yourself a reason why you are putting it in a particular place.

Better still, try to form a connection between the thing in question  and the place where you are putting it. For example, if you put a key in a cup try to imagine yourself drinking with a large key in your hand rather than a cup! When the time comes for you to try to remember where you put the key, then you should at the same time think of the cup and this will help you remember where you put the key. You could also note that the words 'key' and 'cup' both start with the same sound - if you remember one word, then you will be more likely to remember the other one.

Once you've put something away, at intervals afterwards try to think of it, and where you put it. Try to make these intervals a little longer each time.

Recalling in Better Ways

If you have difficulty in finding something which you have put away some time earlier, try to go back in your own mind to when you last remember having the thing. Then, go through step by step what you did and where you were after that. You can also pretend that you are putting the thing away again for the first time, and think of the likely places you would put it. It is often helpful first of all to look very carefully in the most likely places, and later on look in the less likely places.

If you regularly lose items such as your glasses, you could have a pre-prepared system for finding them, and you could write or draw that out and put it in a prominent place. Thus, it may consist of, in the following sequence – Are the glasses in your handbag or coat pocket > are they on a chair or table > are they in the kitchen > are they in the bathroom > are they next to the telephone > are they in the bedroom?

Think of all the items that you have which are similar to the item that has gone missing, and check that it has not been left close to them. Remember to ask someone else whether they know where it might be, or if they can help you find it.

It can sometimes be very frustrating if you cannot find something that you have put away. If you still cannot find it after searching pause and try to relax for a few minutes. Ask yourself how important the thing really is - can you make do with something else for the time being, is there someone who can lend you one, or is it feasible to buy another one?

6. Remembering How To Get Somewhere

Using Memory Aids

There are route-finder websites that will print maps and directions to help you get to a place. Make sure you print out such a map and go over it *before* you set out, and plan any long journey in stages. Landmarks such as hospitals are usually indicated on road maps, and you may find it useful to make a note of these. Some people prefer an actual map of the route, others prefer written directions - choose the one you are happiest with.

You can buy satellite navigation aids, 'Satnavs', that can be fixed in a car. Some Satnavs can also be used when walking about, and most smartphones also have satellite navigation as a feature.

Find out if there is a road sign which you can follow to a particular place near your destination - it is usually easier to do this than following directions to turn right and left several times. Before you set out, it is also wise to take along with you the telephone number of the destination to which you are heading or person you are meeting, and your mobile phone, in case you have to ring someone for further directions.

Some people have difficulties in finding their way around a large building. If you have difficulty in finding your way around a large house, try putting labels or pictures on the doors of some of the rooms to indicate what they are used for. The doors of particular rooms could also be painted in different colours to make them stand out.

Learning in Better Ways

 Allow yourself plenty of time, especially if this is the first time that you have been to this particular place. If the directions you have to follow are quite long, try to split them up into shorter directions and concentrate on one direction at a time. If someone has told you the directions, repeat back in your own words what the person has said to make sure you have got it right, and also if possible repeat it at intervals after that. If you can write down the directions you are given, or record them on a smartphone, all the better. Make a mental picture of going in the particular direction you were given. Ask the person if there is a sign to somewhere else (e.g. a town) that is in the same direction as your destination, as this will be easier to follow than a set of turnings.

If you are going somewhere on foot, look back a few times at various landmarks such as particular shops, so that when you are returning you will be able to recognize places more easily on your return journey. If you are going by car, you could do the same by looking in the rear view mirror a few times.

Recalling in Better Ways

 If you do get lost or have difficulty in following some directions, stay calm and don't panic - just try to work through the directions you have already followed and try to think what other ways you could go. If you have been to your destination before, spend a few minutes thinking back to the directions you followed then.

Finally, don't be afraid to ask someone – e.g. in a petrol / gas station, shop, etc. – for the directions or to phone the place where you are heading / the person you are meeting.

7. Remembering Recent Experiences

Forgetting events that you have personally experienced can be frustrating, and may sometimes be embarrassing in social settings, especially when others have a clear memory for the same events.

 People often complain that they can remember events from their childhood clearly, but cannot recollect more recent events. Often the childhood events have been brought to mind again and again, or were especially meaningful to the person, and this may partly explain why they appear to be so well-ingrained in memory.

There are some general points to keep in mind if you cannot recollect events you have experienced. Firstly, people do vary a lot in how well they can remember events from the past. Some people can recall events from a few years ago in great detail, yet others may have blanks for major events that they have experienced. Secondly, it is natural that unpleasant events may be 'shut out' from the past and are difficult to recollect. Thirdly, in everyday life we are usually concerned with remembering to do things, remembering messages, etc. as these are important for getting things done. Although it can be frustrating if you cannot remember an event that you have experienced some months or years ago, it probably will not significantly affect how you cope in everyday situations.

There are several ways in which it may be possible to make sure that events which you have experienced stick in your memory, or to bring to mind events that may have been forgotten.

It helps if you can regularly rehearse and review an event in the weeks and months after it has occurred – this may involve keeping  a written diary of events, and going over this at a certain time each day or on a certain day each week. If you can add pictures to the diary, all the better. You may even be able to have movie clips of events, or digital photographs that you can replay on a mobile phone, computer or a tablet/iPad. Electronic diary apps exist that allow photos and movie clips to be stored on a smartphone as part of an electronic diary system.

Try to set aside a regular time to review a diary or pictures, ideally with someone who also experienced the same events. Some people keep 'photo montages' of holidays they have been on, or of key family members, in prominent places around the house. If you can get into the habit of occasionally glancing at these photos, this too will help memories for past events stay in mind.

If you cannot bring to mind an event that you experienced some years ago, an event that you may not have had the opportunity to regularly rehearse, then the first thing to keep in mind is to stay calm and not to panic, since panic tends to make it more difficult to bring the event to mind. Memory for the event may come back by itself after a little while. Usually, some hints or cues may bring the event back to mind. Try to think of other events that occurred around the same time, either personally experienced events or news events. If you can talk to someone who also experienced the event, they may be able to give you cues that bring back memories of the event. Looking at photographs is usually a good trigger to bring back 'lost memories'. Remember that it can still be quite normal for a past event not to return to mind, even with cues, so do not worry if this is the case.

8. Useful Memory Aids

In this section, I have described a selection of memory aids, some of which you may find helpful in your particular daily routine. Some of them have already been mentioned in earlier pages. Remember that some of the memory aids described here may not be available where you live. Also, in the case of some aids, especially electronic memory aids, they may be replaced by later models or they may be discontinued.

Stationery Memory Aids

Post-it Note Pads
They come in different colours and sizes, and some are pre-printed with message headings or a check-list. Since regular Post-it notes may fall off after a while, it is useful to know that you can get ones that are 'super sticky' and will stick to a surface for longer. They can be used simply as a reminder to do things – e.g. put on the handle of a door to remind you to take something with you, or on a fridge door to remind you to take something from the fridge. They can also be used as a temporary message pad – e.g. to keep a shopping list, or to write a telephone message. It is often a good idea to keep a notepad or a Post-it Note dispenser with a pen next to the phone.

Post-it Tape
This comes in various colours and widths, from approximately 2.5cm (an inch) to 0.5cm wide. As well as being used to mask over
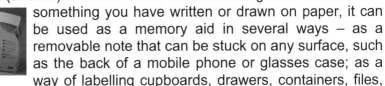
something you have written or drawn on paper, it can be used as a memory aid in several ways – as a removable note that can be stuck on any surface, such as the back of a mobile phone or glasses case; as a way of labelling cupboards, drawers, containers, files, etc; as a written reminder to do things regularly, such as note on a

dry-wipe whiteboard to put out the bins/ garbage on certain days of the week; as a note in the car dashboard to remind you to do things when driving; or, if stuck on a bookmark, a means of keeping notes about parts of a book you are reading.

Notebooks, Diaries and Filofaxes

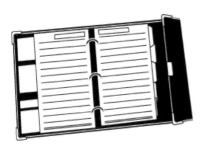

These can be used for entering diary dates, storing names & addresses, and keeping short messages. Pre-printed 'To Do' sheets are available for Filofaxes, and sheets are also available for maps of cities or countries.

Whiteboards and Calendars

Dry whiteboards can be magnetic or non-magnetic, can come in different sizes and can be either blank or pre-printed with days/months. If you use whiteboards or calendars, put them in a prominent place where they can be easily and regularly seen. Anything you write should be in **CAPITAL** letters and in **thick black ink** so that it stands out.

Name Labels

It is easy for people to misplace something or leave it around somewhere. If the item has a label stuck on it, with a name and a telephone number, then it is more likely to be returned to the owner. Labels with written text can easily be printed on a computer and some stationery firms provide such a service. It is also possible to buy pens that can write or print a name and telephone number onto a garment, and labels that can be sewn or ironed on to clothes. If you worry about leaving your own name and home telephone number, you could give that of a friend or just give your work telephone number. In some countries, key clubs exist with whom you can register your keys - a number on the key ring will then alert the finder to contact the key club.

Mechanical Memory Aids

Clocks

It may be worth considering mechanical and electronic clocks that have large clear numbers, and that also display the day and date.

Countdown Timers

These are often found in kitchen stores and are usually inexpensive and simple to use. Four-way timers, which have four separate countdown alarms, may be particularly useful in situations such as when you are cooking several items, each of which takes a different time to cook.

Pill Boxes

Various forms and sizes of pill boxes are available from most chemist or pharmacy stores. Some come with compartments for each day of the week, and for different times in the day. Those with transparent tops, so that you can readily see if a tablet has been taken, are worth considering. Some pill boxes come with alarms attached, to help you remember to take tablets at the right time.

Electronic Storage Aids

Cameras

As well as standard still and movie cameras, wearable cameras

are now available that automatically take still or movie images. The images can usually be easily played back on a mobile phone, a computer, TV or tablet/iPad. Most mobile phones have a camera feature.

Tape Recorders

Many of these are now digital recording devices, do not use tape, and allow for easy indexing and searching for items on the recorder. It is possible to have separate files for messages relating to the home, items relating to work, etc. Some models also come with alarms, and with the ability to transfer the recording to a computer. Most mobile phones have a voice-recording feature.

Electronic Alarm Aids

Watches

Most digital watches have alarm or reminder features. Smartwatches are also available that can be connected to you mobile phone, so that email and text messages, alarms and diary features, and phone calls are synchronised on both devices. Some Smartwatches have voice recorder and camera features, and some have satnav features that help you find your way about.

Plug-Timers
These are plugs with inbuilt timers that can be set to turn electrical equipment on and off at certain times of the day, in case you forget.

Locating Devices

Electronic tagging devices are available that can be attached to an electronic receiver that you may tend to lose, such as keys or a TV remote control. When you press a button on an electronic transmitter, you will get a signal that helps you locate the missing item. Some electronic devices will also give out a signal when you are more than a certain distance away from an object, and this may help if you are often losing things by leaving them behind. Some of these location detection devices can be linked to your mobile phone by installing specific apps.

Telephones

Landline Phones

Most phones have memory storage features, such that you can phone a stored number by pressing a single button. Choose those phones that also have a number display feature, so that you can see the number that you are dialling. 'Photophones' are also available - a number can be programmed to match a photo of a friend, relative or a place such as your local hospital. When the photograph is pressed, the number will automatically be dialled.

Mobile Phones

 Most mobile phones have smartphone features that not only have inbuilt diary and photo/voice recorder systems but also allow for reminder apps and other memory apps to be downloaded. There may also be other features present, such as a still camera, a movie camera and/or a voice recorder that could be of help in coping with memory difficulties.

Navigation Aids

 You can buy satellite navigation aids, 'Satnavs' that can be fixed in a car - they tell you where you are on a map and provide spoken messages as to how to get to a destination. Some of these satnavs can also be used when walking about and many smartphones now have satellite navigation as a feature or which can be downloaded as an app.

9. Frequently Asked Questions

Memory lapses are common. Here are some of the common questions that people ask, and some possible answers.

Q-1 How can I remember where I have put my glasses?

✓ Attach a chain or cord to your glasses and wear this around your neck.
✓ Wear a shirt with a pocket and put your glasses case in the pocket. Stick a name and address label on the glasses case in the event of it being mislaid.
✓ Last thing at night, get into the habit of putting your glasses in a set place.
✓ Keep a spare pair of glasses somewhere else - e.g. near the television, in the car etc.

Q-2 How can I remember to take my tablets, and check to make sure that I have taken them?

✓ Use the reminder system on a smartphone or smartwatch that will go off to remind you to take tablets, together with a transparent 'dosset' pillbox that allows you to see at a glance whether you have taken your tablets.
✓ Try to take your tablets before you carry out a regular activity – such as brushing your teeth, watching a regular TV programme, before a certain meal, etc. Put a Post-It tape next to a kettle or coffee maker, if you regularly drink tea or coffee, and record on the tape when you have taken your medication.

Q-3 How can I remember to take something with me when I leave the house?

✓ Keep it near the front door, so that you will see it when you are about to leave.

✓ Write the name of the item on a strip of Post-it Tape or 'super-sticky' Post-it note, and stick that to the front door.

✓ Keep it with something that you know you will be taking out with you - e.g. near a purse or brief case.

✓ Near to the front door, you could put a motion-sensitive device that plays a recorded message when someone goes by, and that message could be your reminder if you have to regularly take particular items.

Q-4 How can I remember to watch a TV programme at a particular time or listen to a particular radio programme?

✓ Store a message alarm in your mobile phone.

✓ Write the name and time of the TV/radio programme on a Post-it note, and put it on the front of your TV or radio.

✓ Some television or broadband companies allow you to programme reminders into your TV.

Q-5 How can I remember a message that I have been given?

✓ Write it down on a Post-it Note and stick it on your fridge door or on a whiteboard.

✓ Repeat the message as soon as you have been given it to make sure that you have got all the information. Repeat it again several times in your own words, leaving longer intervals in between repetitions.

✓ Make associations to make the message more meaningful.

Q-6 I don't enjoy reading any more because I keep forgetting the plot in the book. How can I improve this?

✓ There is no easy answer to this question, and it may be better to avoid reading long or complicated novels.

✓ You may find that you can still enjoy shorter books or ones with illustrations, or books that you read before, perhaps in your childhood.

✓ One way to keep track of what you are reading is to keep notes as you read, perhaps on Post-it Tape that is stuck onto a bookmark or at the back of the book. When you pick up the book again, you can refer to the notes that you have made.

Q-7 *My problem is not one of remembering, but of unpleasant memories intruding into my mind – how can I forget them?*

✓ There may be understandable reasons why such highly emotional memories keep entering your mind, and you may find it useful to seek specialist help for this. If you see a therapist, you may be taught ways in which to reframe such memories, so that you see past events in a different light, and so that they do not have the same highly intense emotional value.

✓ You may be encouraged to refocus your attention to other more pleasant memories. Bringing these happy memories regularly to mind may also help to improve your mood state and self-confidence.

Q-8 *I have difficulty learning how to use new gadgets...what can I do to help?*

✓ Break down the learning into parts, and learn each part, one at a time. Overlearning each part, with lots of repetitions, will help.

✓ Have key parts of the instructions written down on a card such that they are easy to follow. Place the card next to the gadget in question and try to regularly look at it, perhaps testing yourself from time to time once you have learned the instructions well.

10. Resources for Memory Improvement

(This listing is not meant to be detailed or exhaustive, nor meant to be an endorsement of information in the sites. In addition, some web sites may lapse over time)

www.memory-key.com
Range of topics relating to memory, including memory improvement

www.memorylossonline.com
Newsletters about memory, the site being related to the memory research lab at Rutgers University, USA

alzheimers.org.uk/site/scripts/documents.php?categoryID=200344
The UK Alzheimer's Disease Society, who produce a number of resources to support people with memory difficulties

www.braininjuryhub.co.uk/information-library/memory
The UK Children's Trust, who provide advice on helping children with brain injury cope with memory difficulties

www.cogassist.com
A listing of websites and resources for assistive technology that may help cognitive and psychological functioning

http://www.helpguide.org/articles/memory/how-to-improve-your-memory.htm
Some general advice and tips on helping to ensure that memory lapses do not occur and strategies to improve memory

www.rehab-booklets.com
Booklets that cover a range of difficulties that patients may experience if they have suffered a brain injury or brain illness, or if they find themselves under par for other reasons.

Berry E, Booth M. (2014). *Memory problems after an acquired brain injury*. Salford Royal NHS Trust. [**34 pages**]. Can be downloaded from **http://tinyurl.com/hko3cfc**

Clare L, Wilson BA (1997). *Coping with memory problems*. Thames Valley Test Company (available from www.amazon.co.uk). [**63 pages**]

Baxendale, S. (2014). *Coping with memory problems*. Sheldon Press. [**119 pages**]

Budson A, O'Connor M. (2016). *Seven steps to managing your memory*. Oxford University Press. [**312 pages**]

11. TEN TOP MEMORY TIPS

TAKE IT EASY

1. Try not to do too many things at once. Reduce demands on your memory, perhaps by doing fewer activities or sharing tasks with a family member or an assistant at work. You may have been a perfectionist in the past, and you may find it helps to lower your expectations.
2. Anxiety, depression, tiredness, pain, lack of sleep, alcohol, recreational drugs and some medications can affect memory, so try to control these factors where possible. Try to have a positive frame of mind. Some people find relaxation or meditation techniques of value. Have activities that you find easy and enjoyable as part of your daily routine. Take regular breaks to help prevent fatigue setting in. Regular exercise, 'social sports' (where you mix with others) and weight control can contribute to good health and to a better memory.
3. If you do forget something, don't get too upset about it. Stay calm and wait for a while – what you have forgotten may come back by itself. Learn any lessons as to why you were forgetful on this occasion, so that you make memory lapses less likely to occur in the future.

BE WELL ORGANIZED

4. Keep to a fixed routine, with set activities at set times of the day, and on set days of the week. This will mean that you are more likely to remember to do things.
5. Be organized – have a place for everything, and put back everything in its place. Consider putting labels on drawers, cupboards, containers or files. Use paper-based or smartphone-based or computer-based diary systems. If you use several systems, try to make sure they are synchronised with each other.

CONCENTRATE AND USE STRATEGIES

6. Try not to let your mind wander – keep on track. Be especially careful to concentrate when you are travelling about. If you are often leaving things behind in a room or on public transport, get into the habit of having a final check – 'Look before you Leave'.
7. If you have to do something, do it now rather than later, when it may get lost from your memory – 'Do it Now'.

8. If you have to remember something such as a message or a name, go over it in your mind at increasing intervals. Regularly bringing something to mind ('recall practice') has been shown to result in better memory. If you are forgetful for recent holidays that you have had, keep a written or photo-based diary or video diary, perhaps using your mobile phone. Go over that diary at regular intervals, such as last thing at night or at the weekend. On a wall or display board, you could also have photographs of recent holidays or of key names that you often forget.

9. Try to find meaning in things you have to remember – e.g. by making associations or by linking things together, such as grouping grocery items that go together if you have to remember things to get from the supermarket. If you have to remember to do something later in the day, such as buy milk from the supermarket on the way home from work, try to associate an image of a carton of milk to something you will encounter near to that time, such as your car, or a road near the supermarket.

USE MEMORY AIDS

10. Use memory aids – such as magnetic whiteboards, Post-it notes, check-lists, notebooks, diaries, calendars, alarm timers, smartphones and smartwatches. They can help you to remember messages and help you remember to do things at the right time. Remember that a family member, a friend or a colleague at work can also be a good memory aid! If you have a smartphone, there are many apps that can be helpful as reminders, such as apps that help you remember to take your medication or where you have put things or how to get to somewhere.

12. GREAT MINDS ON MEMORY

I hear and I forget. I see and I remember. I do and I understand.

Confucius

Of two men with the same outward experiences and the same amount of mere naïve tenacity, the one who THINKS over his experiences most, and weaves them into systematic relations with each other, will be the one with the best memory.

William James

When I was young, I could remember anything.....whether it happened or not.

Mark Twain

A wise man deliberately forgets many things.

Mahatma Gandhi

Son, always tell the truth. Then, you'll never have to remember what you said the last time.

Sam Rayburn

The advantage of a bad memory is one can enjoy several times the same good things as if it were the first time.

Nietzsche

Happiness is good health and a poor memory.

Ingrid Bergman

A diplomat is a man who remembers a woman's birthday but never remembers her age.

Robert Frost

The palest ink is better than the best memory.

Chinese Proverb

A retentive memory is a good thing, but the ability to forget is the true token of greatness.

Elbert Hubbard

The true art of memory is the art of attention.

Samuel Johnson

When you were young and in love, you remembered every little detail, months later, without any effort at all. When you listen to a politician speak, you forget every little detail, minutes later, without any effort at all. That's memory.

Can't Remember Who

Printed in Great Britain
by Amazon

45568611R00025